MINDWORKS

Twenty-five advanced English activities for junior secondary students

PETA HEYWOOD

DOUGLAS McCLENAGHAN

SALLY TROTTER

ILLUSTRATED BY

ROB HEYWOOD

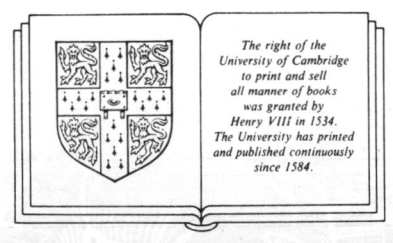

Cambridge University Press

Cambridge

New York   Port Chester   Melbourne   Sydney

Acknowledgement

Published by the Press Syndicate of the University of Cambridge
The Pitt Building, Trumpington Street, Cambridge CB2 1RP, UK
40 West 20th Street, New York, NY 10011-4211, USA
10 Stamford Road, Oakleigh, Victoria 3166, Australia

©Cambridge University Press 1991

First published 1991

Printed in Australia by Capitol Press Pty. Ltd.

*National Library of Australia
cataloguing in publication data:*

Heywood Peta
  Mindworks: twenty-five advanced English activities for junior secondary students.
  ISBN 0 521 42456 9.
  1. English language – Composition and exercises – Juvenile literature. I. Heywood, Peta. II. Trotter, Sally.
  III. McClenaghan, Douglas. IV. Heywood, Rob.

428.076

A catalogue record for this book is available from the British Library.

ISBN 0 521 42456 9. paperback

To the team spirit which helped produce this book and made it fun, and to that same spirit in our classrooms — where everyone wins.

Contents

About this book	iv	I'll always remember	27
Note to students	vii	A quiet place	30
Personal details	1	The good things in life	32
You make the difference	2	Collections	34
My personal emblem	4	How did you feel?	36
A believable story	6	Five steps to writing a first draft	38
My place in the world	8	True colours	40
Wisdom of the ages	10	Creating a mystery	42
A noisy place	12	The other side	45
Hey, listen!	14	A different point of view	48
The form's the thing	16	Dear ...,	50
One perfect day	18	A beautiful place	52
Worries and other nasties	20	The perfect gift	54
Mapping a dream	22	*Mindworks certificate*	56
Creating stories	23		

About this book

Mindworks is an invitation to students to record some of their experiences, observations, hopes and ideas. It provides an opportunity for them to become better at reading, reflecting, revising and thinking, as well as the chance to make a book which could become one of their most precious possessions.

THE ACTIVITIES

As in its predecessor, *Thoughtworks*, each activity in *Mindworks* is designed as a self-contained exercise which requires students to use, and therefore improve, their imaginative, observational and reflective skills as they develop their competence in reading, writing and critical evaluation.

Mindworks is an activities book which draws on each student's own experiences so that it caters for the widest variation in cultural and personal background. It can be used with all ability levels and cultural groupings. As the students share ideas and work together in groups they will have the opportunity to experience what it is like to belong to a writing community, to become members of what Frank Smith has called 'The Literacy Club'.

In writing *Mindworks* our intention has been to provide a variety of activities which release teachers from the full-time role of instructor. This makes time available in which to become familiar with the particular strengths and weaknesses of students and to work with them to develop their skills.

Each activity has a definable end and can be clearly assessed as either *complete* or *incomplete, well done* or *carelessly done*. In all cases the important questions to ask of students are: *Did you complete the activity? Is it your best work?* The teacher's encouragement for students to become experienced in making these judgements for themselves is supported in *Mindworks* by the requirement to note the completion date of each task and regular opportunities for reflection.

Students will be helped to develop competence in editing, revising and shaping their writing by preparing each piece for the space provided. Working from the first draft to finished product is best achieved by using the *Mindworks Notebook* (described on page vii) so that initial work can be expansive and exploratory, rather than tight and restricted. However, sometimes more space than has been provided is necessary for a finished piece and in this case creative problem solving is encouraged.

ORGANISATION

We recommend that:
- students work through this book in the order in which it is presented.
- before writing anything in these pages students work it out in their *Mindworks Notebook* which is explained in the letter to the students. The aim is to let students experience the process of composing, revising, discarding and rewriting as they craft each piece of writing.
- the teacher looks after *Mindworks* during the year. Exactly how class time is used is a decision for the teacher, perhaps in consultation with the students.
- that a regular session be devoted each week to using *Mindworks*. This will allow students to enjoy the social aspects of working on the same project and will provide a regular framework in which the work can take place.

AUDIENCE

An important audience for *Mindworks* activities is the students themselves, now and in the future. It can also include their classmates, family, friends and students in other classes, as well as their teacher.

It is rewarding to provide a varied audience for students' work, hence our focus on showing work to others. Appreciative and supportive audiences are more helpful to inexperienced writers than are those who seek only to criticise.

Mindworks can be displayed, along with other work, at parent-teacher meetings and will provide concrete evidence of the students' achievements. Such displays can provide support for the teacher's work, and be a talking point for parents and other visitors.

LEARNING

Mindworks is based on the following beliefs.
- We learn by transforming one thing into something else (a problem into a challenge, a dream into a story) — a process which involves creative thinking at many levels.
- Language competence occurs as we talk, listen, read and write for meaningful outcomes.
- The most important thing that students make is *meaning* — meaning about the world and their place within it. Making meaning is a lifelong process and is enhanced when young people, from an early age, are required to observe and reflect on themselves and their surroundings.
- Every student has a story to tell and classrooms are important places for these stories to be shared.
- A student's best work, whatever this may be, needs to be received with a focus on the achievements, rather than the omissions or mistakes, if he or she is to continue to learn with confidence.

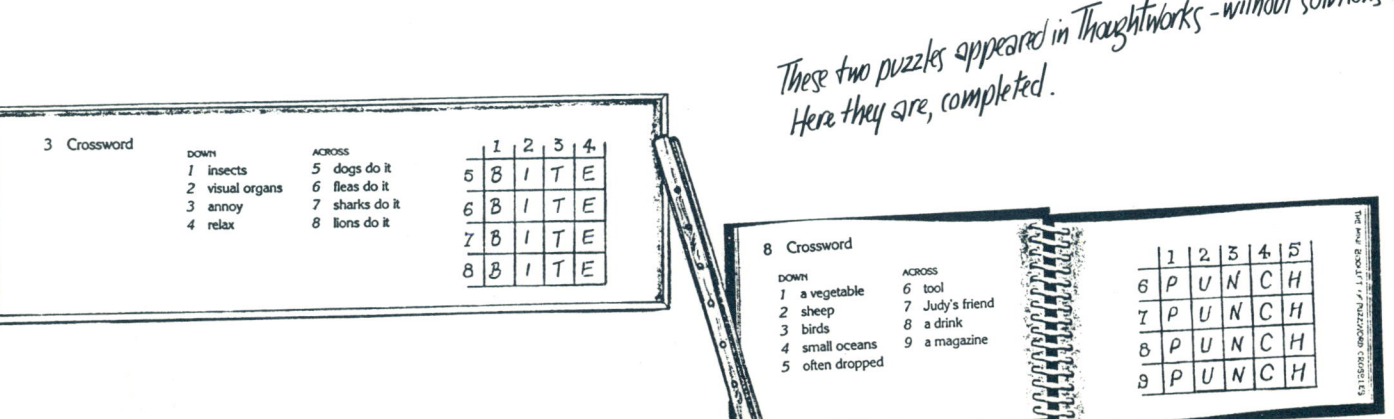

These two puzzles appeared in Thoughtworks — without solutions. Here they are, completed.

Here is a choice of labels for your Mindworks Notebook. Photocopy (either/both), colour and decorate (it/them), and paste (it/them) on your Notebook cover.

Note to students

This book is unfinished. It will be completed when you have added your stories, ideas, colours, pictures and other embellishments. In the beginning it looks the same as all the other copies of *Mindworks*. When it is finished it will be unique, the only one of its kind, the one which is yours.

Mindworks may look simple and easy to do. It is. The challenge it presents is for you *to do your best* and to create a finished book of which you are proud.

We recommend that you:

1 **Make a Mindworks Notebook**
   Because *Mindworks* is for your *best* work, you will need another place for your preliminary planning and writing.
   We suggest that you buy a large notebook to be your *Mindworks Notebook*. Find one you will enjoy using; there are several to choose from, such as those with blank, lined or coloured paper, hard or soft covers, or spiral binding.
   On the next page is a label which you can copy and stick on the cover of your *Mindworks Notebook*.
   Not all that you write in this Notebook will end up as 'finished' writing. You may decide not to continue working on some drafts or to completely alter others. It is also likely that you will notice a difference between the drafts in your Notebook and the final copies you put in *Mindworks*. This difference will increase as you become more skilled at refining your writing and ideas.

2 **Have the tools for the job**
   Writing is a craft and the basic tools you will need while working on this book include: dictionaries, thesauruses, *Mindworks Notebook*, pens, pencils, timers. Check that they are available to you.
   We recommend you use coloured pencils, rather than felt pens, in this book. If possible, try out a few different types of pencils to see which ones give the most pleasing results on this paper.

3 **Understand the process of writing**
   There are two distinctive stages writers go through to produce their best work. These are *creating* and *refining*. You need to do both: create first, then refine.

The *Mindworks Notebook* is where much of your creating will be recorded and developed. *Mindworks* itself will be a collection of your refined writing. When you have finished each activity and feel it is the best you can do at this stage, record the date in the space provided.

Mindworks will reflect your ideas and skill at this stage of your life. It will be a record of the best you can do *now*. It will be there for you to keep for yourself and to share with others when you choose.

Rob, Sally, Douglas and Peta.

RISK

To reach out to another
Is to risk showing your true self
To place your ideas, your dreams,
   your feelings
before people, is to risk appearing
   the fool.

To love is to risk being heartbroken
To hope is to risk despair
To succeed is to risk failure.

But risks must be taken
because the greatest failure in life
is to risk nothing
The person who risks nothing
Does nothing,
Is nothing.

They may avoid suffering and sorrow
But they cannot learn
Learn to live, feel, change, love, grow.
Chained by certainty,
They are slaves,
They have no freedom
For only a person who risks is
   free.

Christine Adamson, Age 15

MINDWORKS Inc. — PERSONAL DETAILS

NAME _____
ADDRESS _____
_____ POSTCODE _____
TELEPHONE (___) _____
HEIGHT _____ WEIGHT _____
AGE _____ DATE OF BIRTH _____
COUNTRY OF BIRTH _____
CITY OR TOWN / VILLAGE _____
DISTINGUISHING FEATURES _____
_____
SHOE SIZE _____ HAT SIZE _____
CLOTHES SIZE _____
FAVOURITE CLOTHES _____
_____
No. OF TEETH _____ No. OF FILLINGS _____
EYE COLOUR _____ HAIR COLOUR _____
SKIN COLOUR _____ FAVOURITE COLOUR ___
FAVOURITE FOOD _____

FAVOURITE AUTHOR _____
FAVOURITE SPORT _____
FAVOURITE FILM _____
FAVOURITE SINGER OR GROUP _____
ECTOMORPH ☐ MESOMORPH ☐ ENDOMORPH ☐
BLOOD TYPE _____ ALLERGIES _____
IN CASE OF EMERGENCY CONTACT _____
_____
_____ TELEPHONE _____
IMPORTANT DATES _____
_____
_____
_____
_____
IMPORTANT TELEPHONE NUMBERS _____
_____
_____
_____
CLUBS / GROUPS I AM A MEMBER OF _____

THE PEOPLE I LIVE WITH ARE _____
_____
_____
_____
MY FAVOURITE PEOPLE ARE _____
_____
_____
MY STAR SIGN IS _____
FAVOURITE PLANT OR TREE _____
OTHER INTERESTING INFORMATION _____
_____
_____
_____
FAVOURITE MUSIC _____
MUSICAL INSTRUMENT/S I PLAY OR WOULD LIKE TO PLAY

PASTE PHOTO OF YOURSELF HERE

MINDAROID

COMPLETION OF THIS PAGE
YEAR _____ MONTH _____
DATE _____ DAY _____ TIME _____

CONFIDENTIAL — ALMOST. CAN ONLY BE READ BY PERSONS WHO ARE LOOKING DIRECTLY AT THIS PAGE AT THIS MOMENT

A MINDWORKS / BRAINTHOUGHT PRODUCTION

You make the difference

Date completed ....

Life is full of challenges and we can choose to meet them or run away from them. We can also set challenges for ourselves.

Examples:

Challenges life throws up

dealing with family problems; poverty; a friend leaving the neighbourhood; sickness; starting a new school; talking in front of the class.

Challenges you set yourself

being fit to play A Grade sport; going in a play; doing well at school; learning to sing/play guitar/tap dance/ride a horse.

Sally believed she had a problem: 'For many years I believed I would never be fit and healthy and so I wasn't'.

She chose to turn her problem into a challenge: 'One day I realised that I'd only achieve health and fitness if I did something about it. For me, the first step was joining a gym and exercising three times a week. I have since progressed to more strenuous programs, taken up running and improved my diet. As a result I feel fitter and healthier than I have done for years'.

Sally wrote this story about meeting her challenge.

JUST DO IT

As I walked down the hallway I could hear a radio playing and the clanking of metal. It was a Thursday afternoon. I was at the gym and about to be taken through my first program.

I had been talking for years about doing some exercise and today was the day. John the instructor met me in the assessment room. He showed me a card with a list of my exercises. It was an introduction to the language of gyms — 'lateral pull downs', 'leg pulleys', 'dumbell flys', 'seated dips'. 'Do two sets of these at 25kg with 10 reps', said John.

It took me about fifty minutes to warm up and then go through all the exercises with John explaining what each one was for and the right way to do it. By the end I was exhausted. 'What have I let myself in for?' I wondered. 'Can any of these people actually be enjoying themselves?' One thing was certain — most of them were a LOT thinner than I was.

As I limped back along the hallway I knew that however painful this was, I would be back. I collected my bag and headed for the car. Driving home was agony. I had worked my muscles so hard that my arms quivered and my stomach cramped. My legs could hardly work the pedals. When I arrived home I was so sore I could not walk upstairs and carry my bag at the same time, so I went in and lay down for half an hour to recover.

That was about 18 months ago. Now I am a lot fitter and enjoy working out at the gym. I am also a LOT thinner and this feels good. I have more energy, eat healthier food and am more alert than I used to be. And, I am not scared to meet other challenges — or to set myself new ones — like horse riding!

by Sally Trotter

1. List five challenges you have accepted.

2. List five challenges you would like to take on. They can be big or small, easy or difficult.

3. List five challenges you have called problems and avoided confronting.

4. Read your list to others in your group. Make a note here of any experiences or challenges which you have in common.

5. Choose one of the challenges from your first list, 'Challenges I have accepted'. Write a story about your experience, like Sally did. Use your *Mindworks Notebook* for the first draft and then rewrite it to fit into the space below.

6. Invent three possible titles for this story and ask six other people to tell you which one they prefer. From their responses and your own further thoughts, choose the title you will use.

Reflection

Think of a challenge that until now you have called a problem, and consider ways you can meet it.

My Personal Emblem

Date completed ....

1. Create a unique emblem by decorating each section of the shield with a symbol (drawing or sign) expressing your answers to questions 1 to 7 below.

2. To discover the symbols which best represent your answers, work through the following steps:

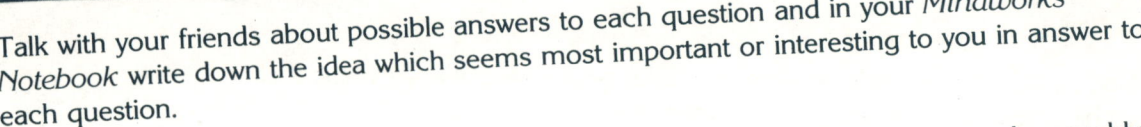

Talk with your friends about possible answers to each question and in your *Mindworks Notebook* write down the idea which seems most important or interesting to you in answer to each question.

Then make up a symbol or drawing which captures each of these ideas. This can be roughly sketched in pencil and the final version completed in the space provided.

Question 6 is different and answered in words. The words could make a sentence.

Question 7 is also answered in words. These words do not make a sentence. They are adjectives which describe the three qualities you have chosen as most important; for example, COURAGEOUS, LONELY, GENEROUS, INTELLIGENT, ATHLETIC, CREATIVE.

THE QUESTIONS

1. What are three things that you do well?
2. What do you want to achieve by the time you are 50?
3. Who is your hero?
4. What is your greatest personal failure to date?
5. What is the thing you like most about your home?
6. What is the personal motto that you live by?
7. What three adjectives best describe you?

Something extra

Ask two people to write, in the space below, the three words that they think best describe you.

PERSON 1 _____ _____ _____

PERSON 2 _____ _____ _____

Reflection

Assess your work by colouring this emblem according to the following code:

Yellow = Excellent

Pink = Better than my usual work

Blue = My usual work

Green = Not my best work

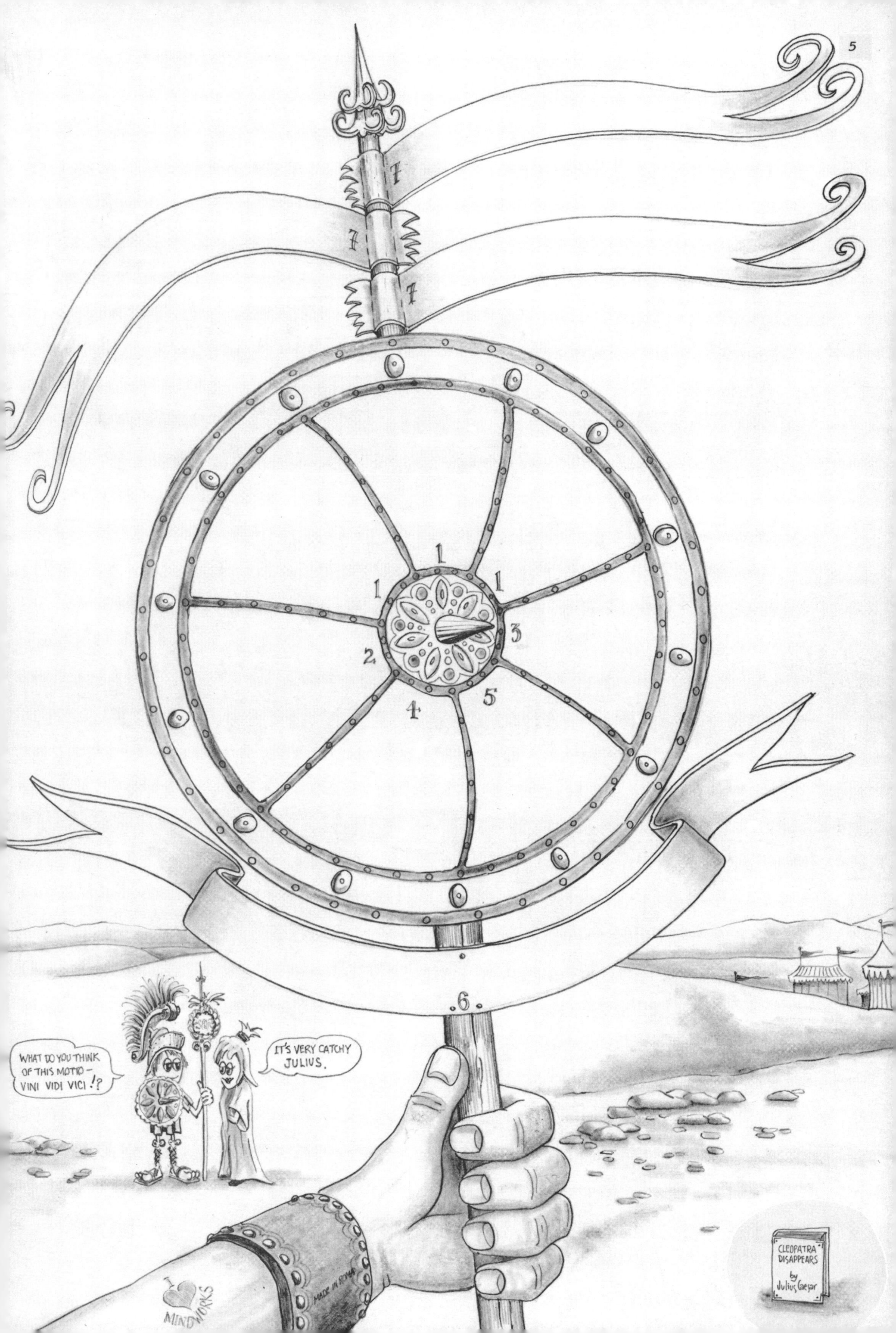

A BELIEVABLE STORY

Date completed ....

1. In your *Mindworks Notebook* write a believable story which includes all of the ingredients from one of the following groups:

a unicorn	an art gallery	a camera
a thunder storm	a lawn mower	a Mah Jong set
12 pink lollies	a professor	a refrigerator
Mount Kenya	10 hair rollers	a Russian dictionary
a potato peeler	a sandcastle	a penguin

   OR / OR

2. An additional challenge is to write using the second person (you) and the present tense. You will be familiar with this if you have read any *"Choose Your Own Adventure"* stories.

3. Read your story to your friends and then copy it into the space provided. If it will not fit, what solutions can you find?

Reflection

'Truth is stranger than fiction'. Do you agree?

My Place in the World

Date completed ....

1. On the next page, draw a map of your neighbourhood using the grid. Show your home and the surrounding area.

2. Draw in the features that are important to you — natural or made by people. Include places of significance; for example, the hairdresser in the next street where you sometimes have your hair cut, the swing in the park from which you fell and broke your collarbone.

   Draw things to scale. For example, your house and the local supermarket will not be the same size on your map.
   Make it colourful.

3. In your *Mindworks Notebook*, describe your house and its occupants. Include the special colours, smells, feelings, noises and other details which distinguish them from all the other houses and people in your neighbourhood. Write for about 30 minutes (non-stop). Add extra time if you take breaks.

4. Using a texta or marker pen, go through your description and underline the features which make your place special.

   Rewrite your description, including all the features which you underlined, so that it fits neatly into the space provided. You may turn it into a poem or an advertisement, or simply cut out as many words as you need to so that it fits the space.

Sample map showing streets: CEREBELUM STREET, WORDBANK WAY, CORTEX PL., LOBOTOMY LANE, COGNITION WAY, COURT, COGITATION BOULEVARD, TINKER WAY, SYNAPSE, THROUGHWAY, MINDWORK, OPTIC LANE, THOUGHT AVENUE, THOUGHTWORKS STREET, HEMISPHERE CRESCENT, LIBRARY LANE. Locations: BOGAN BUILDING COMPANY, DR. CRANIUM'S SURGERY, IMAGINATION INSTITUTE, THOUGHT SPORT COMPLEX, THOUGHTWORKS FACTORY, MINDWORKS FACTORY, BILL POSTER'S PLACE, JACOB'S LADDER MANUFACTURING COMPANY, MILK BAR ("THEY MAKE GREAT THICK-SHAKES, THEY'RE REALLY THICK"), CONSCIOUSNESS SHOPPING CENTRE, IVAN IDEA'S HOUSE, MY FRIEND'S PLACE, PROF. B'S HOUSE, BRAIN TO LET, MIND MUSIC CENTRE, LOBULE LIBRARY, PARAPHRASE PARK, GENE GROVE, SUBCONSCIOUS CREEK ("I FELL IN HERE").

MINDWAY SAMPLE MAP No. C/C 1891 – FAINT EDITION

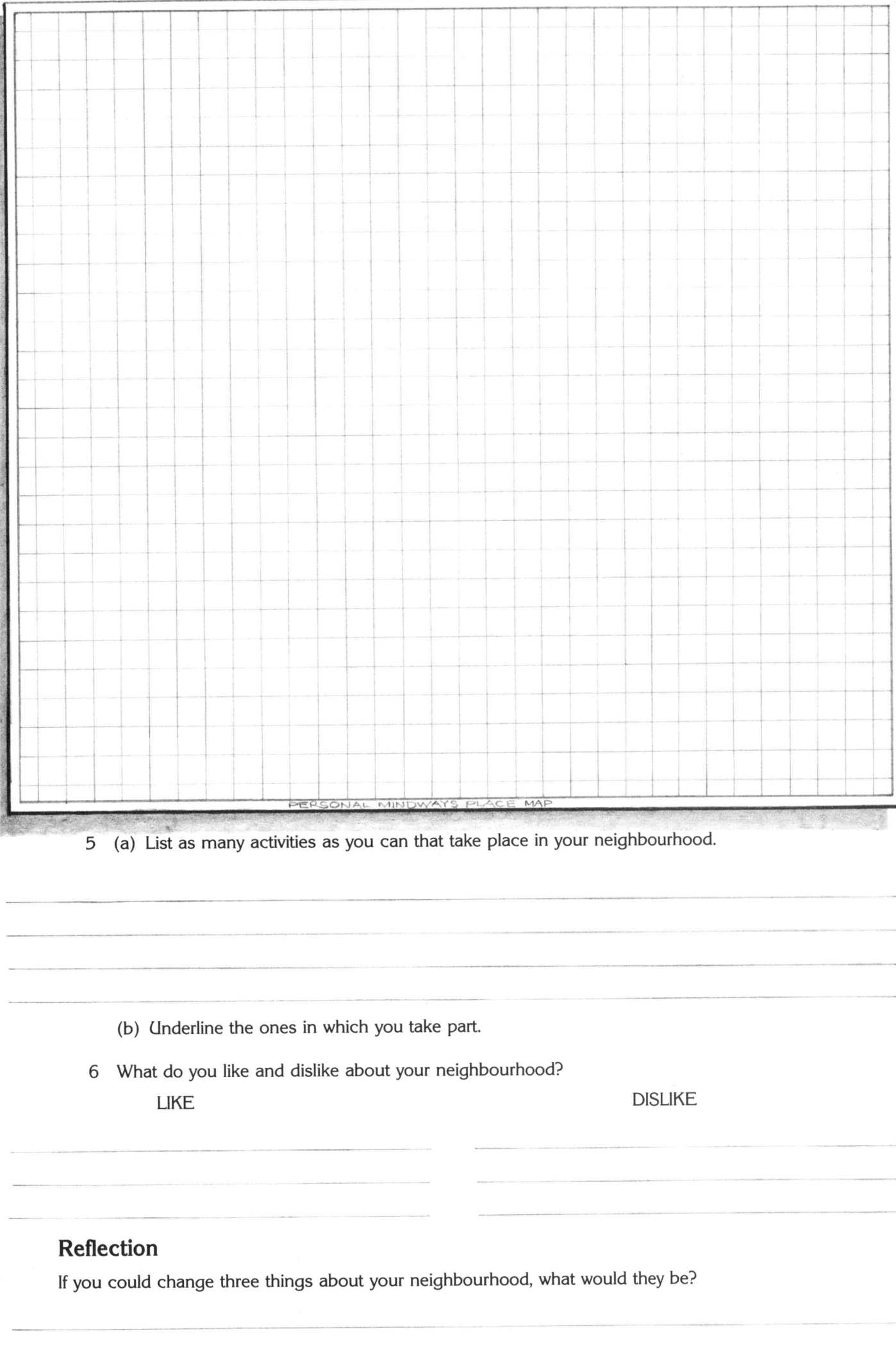

PERSONAL MINDWAYS PLACE MAP

5 (a) List as many activities as you can that take place in your neighbourhood.

_____

_____

_____

(b) Underline the ones in which you take part.

6 What do you like and dislike about your neighbourhood?

LIKE   DISLIKE

_____   _____

_____   _____

_____   _____

Reflection

If you could change three things about your neighbourhood, what would they be?

_____

_____

WISDOM OF THE AGES

Date completed ....

1. Working in groups, match up the halves of each of these proverbs. Join the two halves together with different colours.

You climb more surely	out of a sow's ear.
Empty vessels make	is worth two in the bush.
A bird in the hand	blame their tools.
Look before	the mice will play.
More haste	you leap.
A good pupil	will sink a great ship.
Enough is as good	the most sound.
You can't make a silk purse	makes less speed.
Cooks are not to be taught	you will please no one.
When the cat's away	as a feast.
You can lead a horse to water	shouldn't throw stones.
Bad workers	before you've shot it.
All that glitters	but it pours.
Pride goeth (goes)	but you can't make it drink.
People who live in glass houses	don't make a right.
Two wrongs	is not gold.
Blood is thicker	with honey than with vinegar.
It never rains	than water.
If you try to please everyone	one rung at a time.
A small leak	is not always a good teacher.
You catch more flies	before a fall.
Don't skin a bear	in their own kitchen.

An extra challenge is to write each complete proverb in your *Mindworks Notebook* or make a class poster of the five you think are most relevant to your group.

2. Think about your life and choose an event to which one of these proverbs applies. Using the proverb as the title, write about this event in your *Mindworks Notebook*.

3. Edit your story so that it fits in the space provided or add more paper to fit your story.

Reflection

There is another saying: 'Wise people learn from others' mistakes; fools learn from their own'. If this is true, are you wise or foolish? Record your rating on the 'Wiseguide'!

A NOISY PLACE

Date completed ....

Writing about something you have experienced and therefore *know* is often easier than writing about something about which you are ignorant. A mixture of experience and imagination is one clue to writing well.

In this activity you can use your experience and your imagination.

1. Choose a noisy place to visit. Take your *Mindworks Notebook* and spend 30 minutes there listening to the sounds and watching what is going on. Notice what you feel and what you remember.
   Write your observations in your *Mindworks Notebook*.

2. Use that place as the setting for a story. The story can be about anything you choose. The challenge is to include the sights, sounds and feelings you have recorded.
   Write the first draft of the story in 20 minutes. This can be done either at the place or after you have spent about ten minutes creating a picture of it in your imagination.

3. Read your story to two other people and then put it away for two days. On the third day read it to yourself and make any changes which you think will improve it.
   Write the finished version in the space provided. Give it a title.
   Decide what type of story you have written and mark it on the chart below.

Something Extra
Rewrite your story as a different type. For example, if you wrote an adventure story, rewrite it as a report.

Reflection
On the 'Mindworks Genrescope' colour in the categories which best describe the type of story you have written.

Hey! My story's more than one type!

So's mine — it's a romance and an adventure!

| ADVENTURE | MYSTERY | ROMANCE | MYTH | TRAGEDY | FAIRY TALE |
| SOAP OPERA | BIOGRAPHY | REPORT | DESCRIPTION | ADVERTISEMENT | DRAMA |

◆ MINDWORKS GENRESCOPE ◆

Did you mark more than one type for your story?

How well do you focus?
Working with a group of friends, answer each of these questions as quickly as you can.

FORM 17 EAR/K9
Please do not dog-ear this form

LISTENING TEST No. I/EER/O

COMPILED BY
AURAL B.
EARLESS

In 1964 twenty-seven students completed this test and by 1982 most of them had almost completely recovered.

1953 a university professor attempted this test... he is now up to question seven.

1. How many birthdays does the average person have?
2. Why can't a man living in Darwin be buried in the Melbourne Cemetery?
3. If you had only one match, and entered a room in which there was a kerosene lamp, a gas stove and a wood fire, which would you light first?
4. Some months have 31 days, others 30; how many months have 28 days?
5. If a doctor gave you three tablets and told you to take one every half hour, how long would they last you?
6. There is a house with four sides to it. It is square in shape. Each side faces south. A bear comes wandering by. What colour is the bear?
7. How far can a deer run into a forest?
8. If a horticulturalist had 19 prize tulips and fungus killed all but 9, how many survived?
9. Divide 30 by a half and add 10.
10. Take two apples from three apples and what do you have?
11. A woman gives a beggar 20 cents. The woman is the beggar's sister but the beggar is not the woman's brother. How is this?
12. Is it possible for a man to marry his widow's sister?
13. Two men are standing in a room looking at a picture of a man on the wall. One man says to the other, while pointing to the picture, 'Brothers and sisters have I none but that man's father is my father's son'. Who is the person in the picture?
14. A girl builds a cube of six large mirrors. She climbs inside before the top mirror is lowered on to the four walls. Each mirror is at right angles to the other, and the structure is in the middle of a paddock. So the six mirrors form the floor, ceiling and four walls of the cube, each fitting perfectly to the other. The girl looks about them; how many reflections of herself can she see?

A MINDWORKS MENTAL MANGLER PRODUCTION

ANOTHER MINDSIGN

In 1937 an African explorer was interrupted while doing this test. He never correctly it, or returned the book.

MEMO

Ivan,
Please hang the signs straight.
Thankyou,
Prof.

In 1937 a trained gorilla completed this test in just three and a half minutes.... and got every answer wrong. He then ate an explorer.

Reflection

How does answering these questions relate to your learning?

THE FORM'S THE THING

Date completed ....

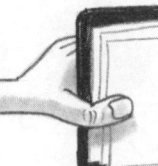
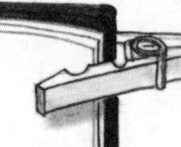

Stories have a beginning, a middle and an end — but not necessarily in that order.

What else determines the form of a story?
Read on for some other ideas.

A PINE MINDSIGN

IDEA 1

In this example, the *length of the words* determines which ones you can use, and hence the form of the story. Start with a one-letter word, then a two-letter word and build up to as many as you can.

Here is an example:

I
go
far
when
using
horses
running
joyously

In your *Mindworks Notebook* work out some examples of your own and include the best ones here.

IDEA 2

In this case, the *first letter of each word* determines which words can be used and in what order. The story has 26 words, the first word beginning with A, the second word with B, and so on.

Here are two examples:

A beaver can dig every Friday going home idiotically: juggling kangaroos, leaping mountains noisily or perhaps quietly, rapidly sneezing terribly under Volkswagens while x-raying yabbies zoologically.

Amanda Bear consistently dropped eggs from great heights in John's kitchen leaving many nasty odd patches. Quickly running she tripped, uncovering Vivian's wicked xenophobic youthful zeal.

Rewrite here the best story you can compose using this model.

A FORMAL MINDSIGN

IDEA 3

Key words can also determine a story. Go through a magazine or newspaper and cut out ten words that appeal to you. Use them all in a story of not more than 200 words which you draft in your *Mindworks Notebook*. When you are happy with your result, write the story on a poster, paste the words around it and display it in your classroom. Alternatively, you could do this on a good piece of paper which you can paste in here.

SIGN BY RUSTICMIND

IDEA 4

The *way a story is told* or narrated also determines the form. From magazines, cut out pictures of each of the following:

- a place
- something wet
- something purple
- an insect or animal
- something that flies or floats

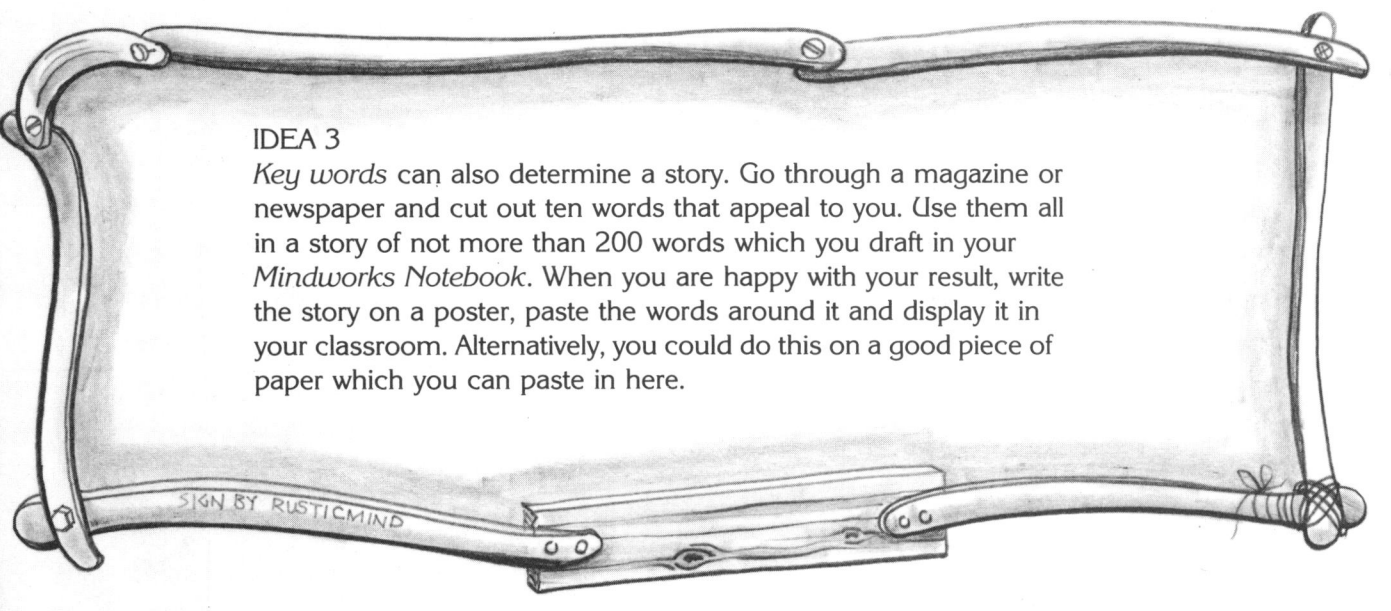

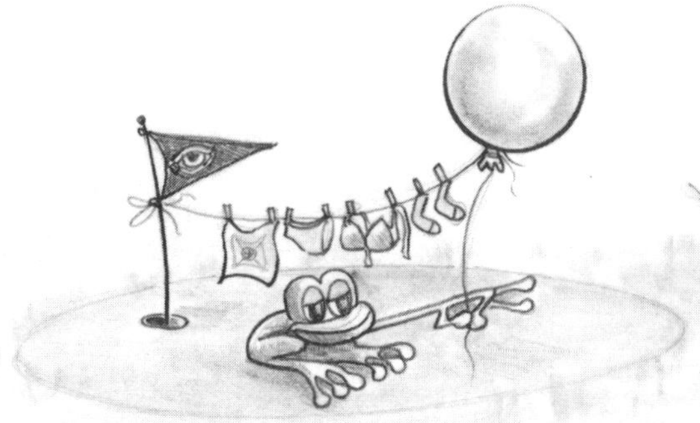

i Write a story in which you include each of the items you have cut out. Your challenge is to write this story from the point of view of ONE of the items. For example, it could be told from the point of view of a grasshopper, a wet towel, a purple flower, a tennis court or a sandy beach.

ii Rewrite your story on an attractive sheet of paper and decorate it with the pictures or drawings of the pictures. Paste it into this book or display it in your classroom.

A FLEXITEAR MINDSIGN

iii Think about how differently the story might be told from the viewpoint of one or all of the other items.

A FLEXITEAR MINDSIGN EXTENSION

Reflection

Which of the above activities did you enjoy most and why?

ONE PERFECT DAY

Date completed ....

I am sitting on the jetty with my fishing rod in the water. My feet are dangling over the end and my jeans are rolled up. The line is out fairly deep and has a small yabby on the hook. I am watching the end of the rod and it is moving back and forward slightly. I stand and pick up the rod. As I start to wind it in I feel little tugs. It's a redfin.

Stuart

I open the letter. It's from Greg Norman and he wants to play golf with me! I meet him on the golf course and when I tee off I hit the ball 200 metres; when Greg tees off he hits the ball five hundred. I ask him if he will teach me to hit as far as he can and he says yes. At the second tee he shows me how he hits the ball. I try to do the same but the ball only goes about three-quarters of the distance Greg's does. He says to me that it was a great shot. By the end of the day I can hit that ball twice as far as I could before. It was a perfect day.

Bart

Today is my perfect day. My book has been published. It is a great feeling to look at it and to think that I wrote it. It hasn't gone on sale yet and I'm a bit scared that people won't like it, but I think it's good. It's about a magical world with monsters, and heroes who save the world. I can't believe it; I've published a book. I've always wanted to do that.

Brett

I am on a farm, our friends' farm. It is sunny and they are teaching me how to ride their horse. I learn quickly. They take me down to the back paddock and there is a horse I haven't seen before. They tell me that it is mine and they will help me look after it and teach me how to ride.

Kathryn

I am in a plane with four other people. Two men and two women. The pilot is telling us about when to jump and at what level to jump. I have never parachuted before but have waited all my life to do it. My stomach has butterflies and I am shaking. The other people are new to it too. Looking at their faces I can feel their excitement, but at the same time I can sense their fear. The plane takes off. I sit down and talk to the woman beside me. In another couple of minutes I will be falling to the ground. The man in charge stands up. The red light goes on. I walk over to the doorway.

The fear is building up inside me. I feel like I'm going to be sick. I convince myself to take the plunge. 'Jump, Jump!' says the man in charge. I put one foot forward. The wind blows in my face. I jump. I am falling fast. Cars look like ants, skyscrapers in the distance look like normal houses. I pull the cord. Then I panic. 'What if the cord breaks?' It doesn't. The parachute opens. All the rest is easy. I am having fun. Then I land, on my knees. It hurts. But it is worth it. I know I will be parachuting again.

Ben

1 Take some time to imagine yourself in the future on a perfect day in your life. Picture yourself doing something you love which turns out perfectly for you.

What do you look like? How old are you? What are you doing? What do you see when you look around you? What sounds do you hear? Is anyone with you? Who? What feelings do you have in this lovely place? What is happening?

This can be done with the whole class, with a few friends or by yourself. Take at least ten minutes to imagine the scene and make it perfect for you.

2 In your *Mindworks Notebook* describe your perfect day as if it is happening as you write.

3 Rewrite your story in the space provided. Use *One Perfect Day,* or think of a better title.

Reflection

What days from your past could be classified as 'perfect'?

What is perfection?

WORRIES AND OTHER NASTIES

Date completed ....

WORRY BOX No. EC1

GUATEMALAN CHILDREN HAVE SIX TINY 'WORRY DOLLS' WHICH THEY KEEP IN A BOX. BEFORE GOING TO SLEEP EACH NIGHT THEY TELL A WORRY TO EACH OF THESE DOLLS.

WHAT WORRIES DO YOU HAVE? LIST THEM IN THIS BOX.

1 Read Emma's story about *her* worries.

The Mistake We Cannot Make

I am worried about the Greenhouse Effect. Even if we will all die one day does that mean that the Earth has to die with us? That there will be nothing to pass on to our children?

I have longed to be able to have children of my own and I am now scared that this will not be possible.

We're supposed to learn from our mistakes but if we make this mistake no one will learn anything because there will be nothing left.

With this mistake there is no second chance. You might think I am stupid worrying about this but I believe we all need to do what we can to fix this mistake before it is too late.

I will stop using spray cans, I will keep learning what I can do about it and convince others to help as well. I will do what I can to see that the world is safe for the next generation.

162 words

Below are Emma's first and second drafts of this piece. They show the changes she made in her *Mindworks Notebook* after reading it to others and talking about her ideas.

First Draft

~~Everyone says we're going to die, but~~ We will all die one day. ~~D~~does that mean that the Earth has to die with us? ~~so that we can't pass our world on to the new generation?~~ That there will be nothing to pass on to our children?

~~As a child~~ I have longed to be able to have children of my own, ~~but at this rate I don't think I will be able to.~~ and I am now scared that this will not be possible.

I have read about ~~people saying~~ the world ~~will come~~ coming to an end, ~~and have heard people say that our life on earth will end before anything can be done.~~ ~~but I don't think that it is us who will cause this damage.~~ ~~I don't think that what we do every day is taking so much of our life on Earth away. We might be able to slow all of this down, but people keep saying, "Oh it doesn't matter, our life on Earth is going to end before anyone can do anything about it."~~ ~~People say we~~ We are supposed to learn from our mistakes but if we make this mistake no one will learn anything because there will be nothing left to fix.

Start with this.

With this mistake there is no second chance. ~~If you haven't caught on to what I am saying~~ I am ~~talking~~ worried about the Greenhouse Effect. ~~In my own way I understand what is happening.~~ ~~Some people~~ You might say I am stupid worrying about this but I ~~don't care, because at least I am trying to~~ believe we all need to fix this ~~my~~ mistake before it is too late.

Delete

~~It is Not only spray cans that is doing this, but it is many other things as well. I am scared in a lot of ways of what is happening to the Earth. I bet there are a lot of kids my age who wish to grow to be teenagers and then become adults and have children, but if the Greenhouse Effect gets worse, what world will we have to bring our children up in?~~

Not only will I stop using spray cans, I will keep learning what I can do about it and convince others to help as well. I will do what I can to see that the world is safe for the next generation.

325 words

Second Draft

I am worried about the Greenhouse Effect. ~~W~~ Even if we will all die one day ~~.~~ ~~D~~does that mean that the Earth has to die with us? That there will be nothing to pass on to our children? (37)

I have longed to be able to have children of my own and I am now scared that this will not be possible. (23)

~~I have read about the world coming to an end and have heard people say that our life on earth will end before anything can be done.~~ We are supposed to learn from our mistakes but if we make this mistake no one will learn anything because there will be nothing left. With this mistake there is no second chance. (33)

You might think I am stupid worrying about this but I believe we all need to do what we can to fix this mistake before it is too late. (29)

~~Not only will~~ I will stop using spray cans, I will keep learning what I can do about it and convince others to help as well. (42) I will do what I can to see that the world is safe for the next generation.

162

189 words – 27 too many. 50% is 162 words.

2 Writing can be a useful way of solving problems at all times in your life. See how this works by writing in your *Mindworks Notebook* about one of the worries you have listed. Explain why it is a problem for you and suggest some possible ways of handling it.

3 Read through your piece and talk about it with at least two other people. Can you get rid of 50% of the words?

Cutting out unnecessary words helps make a piece of writing balanced, light and interesting. It also helps you see the problem (and the solution) more clearly. In Emma's example, look particularly at the changes to the last paragraph.

4 Check the remaining words for correct spelling and punctuation. Use your dictionary and ask for help when you need it.

5 Go through the piece and underline the most important phrases. Choose one and work it into a title.

6 Copy your story into the space provided.

Something extra
Find out what you can about Gaia.

Reflection

Has your attitude to your worry changed through doing this activity? If you feel happier, maybe you could do this with other worries. If not, who could you ask for help?

Mapping a Dream

Date completed ....

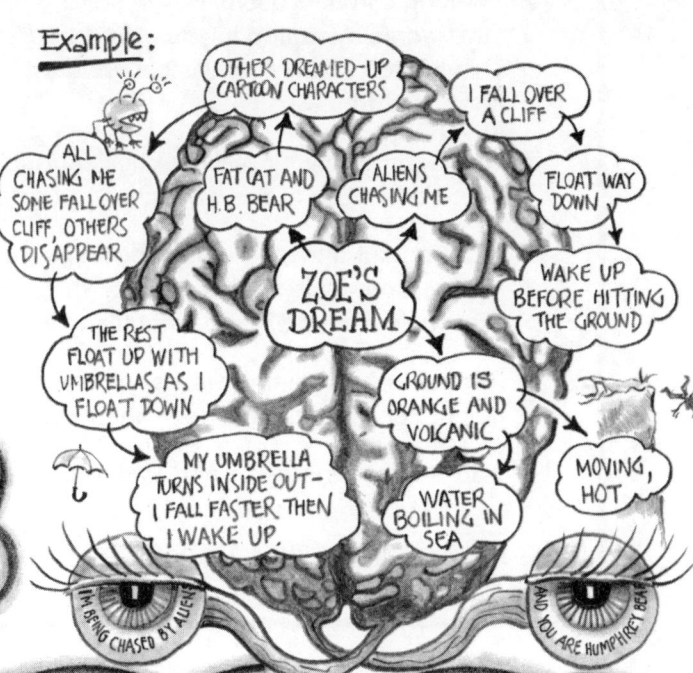

Example:

1. Think of a dream you have had and make a map of the details in the space below. Use colours and draw pictures if this helps to catch the dream.

2. Dreams can be turned into fiction; they are stories you have already composed. In your *Mindworks Notebook*, rewrite your dream as a short story.

3. Edit and improve the story before writing it on the kind of paper you like best and attaching it to this page.

Handy hints for remembering dreams

Get lots of sleep — dream periods get longer and closer together as the night proceeds.

As soon as you wake up, ask yourself 'What was I thinking and feeling?' Keep still and concentrate on this question.

Keep a notebook beside your bed and write down dreams as soon as you wake up: this may happen in the middle of the night as well as in the morning.

Reflection

Making maps for stories is a form of planning which many people find invaluable. When will you next practise this technique?

CREATING STORIES

Date completed ....

1. **PLACES** — Where does your story happen? Look at the picture on pages 24 and 25. Listed below are ten places which are in the picture. Find each one and colour it. Imagine the people who might live in or visit these places.

   - a mixed farm
   - a cave
   - a seaside resort
   - an amusement park
   - mountains
   - a bridge
   - a river
   - the village
   - a city
   - Park Avenue

   List some other places you find interesting.
   ....
   ....
   ....

2. Complete colouring the places in the picture.

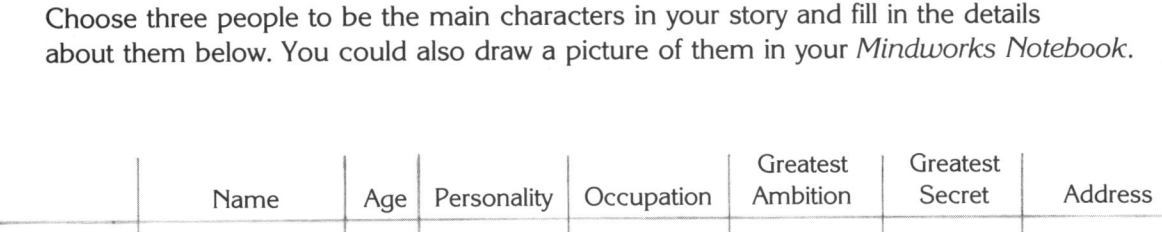

3. **PEOPLE** — Who will be in your story?
   Choose three people to be the main characters in your story and fill in the details about them below. You could also draw a picture of them in your *Mindworks Notebook*.

	Name	Age	Personality	Occupation	Greatest Ambition	Greatest Secret	Address
Character 1							
Character 2							
Character 3							

4. **EVENTS** — What happens?
   Lots of things can happen in stories, such as:

Chases	Expeditions	Adventures	Deaths
Fires	Discoveries	Fights	Parties
Earthquakes	Romances	Births	Ceremonies

   Underline three which you would like to have in your story or add your own. Think about which of your characters will be in the events, why they are involved, and what the result will be.

5. Using some or all of these events and people, write a story which happens in the places in the picture.

   Take the time to do your first draft in your *Mindworks Notebook* and edit it carefully before writing it in the space provided on page 26. If your story is too long, what can you do to give yourself more space in which to write it?

Reflection

Where did your ideas come from?

I'LL ALWAYS REMEMBER

Date completed ....

Here is a challenge. Create a picture in your mind of someone you want to remember, someone who is important to you. Imagine all the details of this person so that they will remain fresh in your memory for years to come.

1   Read the two stories below and think about the person you want to remember and what you could write about them.

MY GRANDPA
by Marzia

I've been to Italy a couple of times in my life to visit my mum's dad and there hasn't been a single time that I was bored listening to him crack jokes or telling me stories of his life. I especially liked the stories of his life in Africa as a lieutenant during the second World War.

I still remember meeting him at the airport at the age of thirteen after not seeing him for three years. He was standing at the bottom of the plane's stairs; he had managed to get in with a special pass because he knew people at the airport. He gave me such a hug that I could feel my bones almost crack. His eyes were shining with joy and he was also very nervous.

He's not very tall, rather smallish but very proportionally built and strong for his age. He has an open and inviting face, always ready to tell or listen to a joke. He's very intelligent and loves talking with people about everything.

He lives in a flat which he shares with his younger sister (my aunty). He has two older brothers as well as seven, yes seven, sisters. He is the oldest of them all.

At home, he started telling me episodes of his life when he was sent to Africa to stabilise political and military influence in the Italian colonies. This is the time in his life he remembers with a hint of nostalgia because he was young and adventurous.

He told me of a time when one of his soldiers was attacked and eaten by a crocodile and they had to go out and look for it. Eventually they shot and killed a huge monster, about five and a half metres long and when they cut it open, they found the remains of the soldier. This happened because the soldier disobeyed my grandfather's orders not to go near the river at night.

I really enjoy listening to stories of his life during the War because somehow every story has a moral or teaches me a lesson.

In Rome, he used to take me with him all the time because he said that living in a big Italian city is a dangerous business and how right he was. With him I learned to cross at a pedestrian crossing (because in Italy it is suicide to cross the street) and especially how to watch out for pickpockets.

I really miss his funny stories and jokes now that I've come back from my holiday. My mum writes to him often to say how are you going because I can't write in Italian. I hope to return soon.

WE ALL NEED FRIENDS
by Sharryn

It wasn't fair. It was always Stephanie. Stephanie was always quiet and very shy. She wouldn't say boo to a ghost. Stephanie was different from the other kids. She'd sit by herself, both in and out of the classroom. Stephanie would never talk to any of the other kids at school. Once I tried talking to her but she didn't seem to want to talk. It was as if she didn't want to have any friends. We went to Blackwood Primary and we were both in Grade Three.

I felt sorry for Stephanie; I wondered what it would be like to be like her, to not have anyone to talk to at school, to be alone.

Then it started. A new girl arrived at school. Her name was Lyndal. Personally I didn't like her. I thought she was a bully and there was something about her that put me off. Lyndal thought she was really good and wasn't much liked by the teachers and a lot of the students.

Lyndal started teasing Stephanie though Stephanie would never say or do anything. I would watch her. She'd just sit there and take it as if she didn't care, as if she didn't have feelings, as if nothing could hurt or offend her.

Lyndal thought it was all a game, a joke. She would say cruel things to her and tease her because she couldn't do things.

'Are we going to have another cry today?' Lyndal would tease.

'Cry baby, cry baby', chorused Lyndal's friends.

'Have you got your nappy on?' Lyndal would say and walk off laughing.

Stephanie just seemed to be more isolated, like in prison, not letting anyone in to be her friend.

Well I was going to try to be her friend and if she didn't want to be my friend I wouldn't force her.

'Hello', I said.

She didn't answer me, just kept eating her lunch.

'My name's Sharryn.'

'Hi', she answered, 'I'm Stephanie'.

Over a couple of weeks Stephanie and I became, I suppose you could say, friends. Not best friends or anything. I didn't know a great deal about her, but I knew her better than anyone else did.

Then Lyndal started teasing her again and had a go at me for hanging around with her. I fought, telling Lyndal to leave her alone. Surprisingly she did.

Stephanie soon left Blackwood Primary. She didn't stay long, only about eight months. Lyndal soon found someone else she could give a hard time to.

Stephanie taught me something but I didn't realise it straight away. Stephanie taught me that at one time or another we all need a friend, no matter who we are.

2. In your *Mindworks Notebook* make a list, or brainstorm as a map, the details you know about *your* special person. It often helps if you talk about the person to other people.

3. Using these ideas write a description or anecdote of the person and explain why you think they are special.

4. We have left a space for your final crafted version of this story. Can you find a photograph which you can use as an illustration?

Reflection

Why did you choose this person to write about? Answer in one sentence.

A QUIET PLACE

Date completed ....

Sometimes we all need a retreat, a place to go to when the noise and clamour of the everyday world is getting us down.

1. Describe a quiet, relaxing place you would choose as your retreat. (It can be real or imaginary.) Before writing, visit that place (either in reality or in your imagination). Take time to look around you and notice the sights, sounds and smells. Be aware of the feelings you have. Describe this place in words and pictures.

2. Write your first draft in your *Mindworks Notebook*. Read it two days later and see if your description brings the place to life for you. Have you used calm and quiet words in your writing? Add some drawings if you can.

3. When you are satisfied with this description, copy it into the space provided.

Reflection

How can you use this quiet place in your life?

THE GOOD THINGS IN LIFE

Date completed ....

Do you spend more time looking at what's good in your life, or what's bad?

When you are with other people is it more pleasant when they talk about what's good, or what's bad for them?

Take some time to think positively about yourself and your life as you do the following exercises.

1. Make a list of everything that you appreciate or are thankful for in your own life. (We hope there's room in the space below. If not, put them in your *Mindworks Notebook*.)

2. Compare lists with your friends.

Briony turned some of her list into a poem.

> I'm thankful for my mum
> Who makes things into fun,
> And also for my dad
> Who cheers me when I'm sad.
> I'm thankful for my friend
> On whom I can depend.
> I'm thankful for our pets,
> Who do things you don't expect.
> I'm thankful for the trees
> Which help the world to breathe
> I'm thankful for my house's warmth
> which keeps me safe in any storm.
> And for the life I lead
> and the food on which I feed.
> But most of all I'm thankful for —
> Being who I am.

So did Ross:

> Firstly I'm thankful for my dog,
> Who brightens the darkest day.
> For my tape recorder,
> Which is music to my ears.
> For computer games,
> That help me to unwind
>   after a hard day's work.
> For puppies which give me joy
> And for my humility,
>   which I can hold on to,
> Even when I am praised.
> For all these I am grateful.

3 Turn your list into a poem or a letter, using as many items as you can and creating a rich picture of the things you treasure in your life.

4 Write it below. Colour and decorate the border to match your feelings.

Reflection
How can you show your appreciation to someone?

COLLECTIONS

Date completed ....

1. What are the sorts of things you have collected in your life?
   List them here — anything, from toys to turtles, boxes to billycarts.

   WE COLLECT SIGNS.

2. Among the things Peta collected were emperor gum caterpillars, swap cards, jacks (knuckle bones from the leg of lamb), marbles, stamps, Dinky toy cars, frogs, tadpoles and cicadas.
   Read her story about cicadas.

HOW I BECAME A CICADAPHILE *
by Peta Heywood

My bedroom was large and one wall was nearly all window. Along this entire wall, beneath the window, was a desk about four metres long. It had book shelves at each end, cupboards and drawers below, and I loved it. Such a large, clear and strong surface had many uses. But what I remember most is using it to display my collection of cicada shells.

During the cicada season I had spent many of my early childhood days saving cicadas from birds. I hated to hear the croak of a cicada as the bird pecked off its legs and then ate the juicy abdomen until finally the croaking ceased. The sound of cicadas was for me a mixture of joy and horror and it was several years before I admitted to the futility of one small girl trying to save the cicada population from being devoured.

In the meantime, I sometimes had as many as 15 rescued cicadas in my care and I came to love the brightness of their colour, the transparency of their delicate wings, the way they could cling on to most surfaces with their thin and scratchy legs.

When I was not saving them I hunted for their discarded shells. I became expert at finding them on the trunks and lower branches of the trees in our neighbourhood. I learned that cicadas spend seven years underground growing to maturity and when they are ready to mate they burrow up to the surface and break out of the shell which has protected them. Their brown, earth-coloured casings split down the back and allow the cicada to emerge. The whole process takes several hours as they have to unfurl their wings and let them dry and become rigid.

They are completely transformed into the bright green, flying creatures I felt compelled to rescue.

They emerge from the ground on summer evenings when they are less exposed to predators and in the mornings the empty shells can be found, still looking like a living creature, clinging to the tree whose roots the crowing cicadas have fed on for years.

I was fascinated with these shells. I sometimes wore one on my clothing as if it was a brooch, or decorated my bedroom with them or just crushed them for fun. Then one season I hunted for them with the intensity and fervour of a true collector. That year I collected over a hundred. The next year I tried to better my total until, in one season, I collected over three hundred shells.

It was a problem storing them. They crushed easily and took up a great deal of space. Then I had a brainwave — the desk! I arranged the shells on the large flat surface as if they were an advancing army. I could not use the desk for anything else, including homework, and the shells became covered with dust and gradually disintegrated. I had to keep the windows closed too — the slightest puff of wind blew them all over the floor. I kept them like that for months.

The next summer I walked past trees without looking at the trunks in case I saw a cicada shell. My interests moved on to other things but each year I am reminded of my collection when the cicada chorus begins.

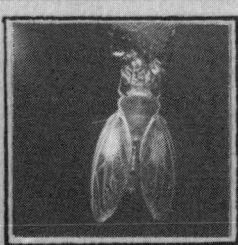

*A made-up word meaning 'one who loves cicadas'. From the Greek 'philos', *friend* and 'phileein', *to love*.

3 Talk to your friends about things you have collected. Decide which one you will write about and complete the first draft in your *Mindworks Notebook* in about 20 minutes.
4 After three days re-read this draft, edit it and rewrite it into this space. Include a title.

Something extra
Give a talk to the class about your collection. Bring some or all of your collection with you to show others.

Reflection
What have you learned from being a collector?

How did you feel?

Date completed ....

1. Think of a time when some strong emotion overwhelmed you. Recall the circumstances and the reactions of those around you.

2. When you have read Douglas' story, think about how you could turn your own experience into a story.

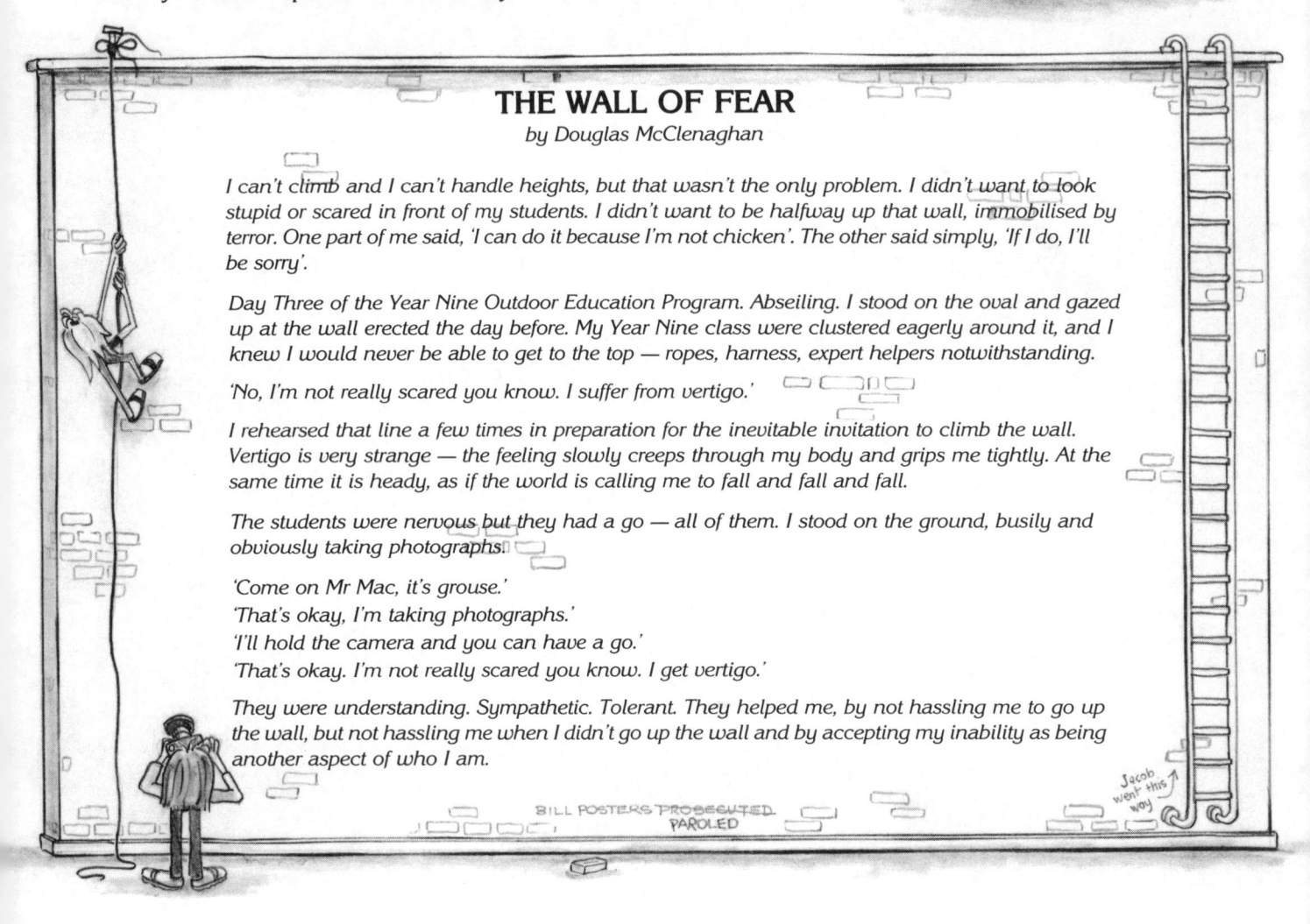

THE WALL OF FEAR
by Douglas McClenaghan

I can't climb and I can't handle heights, but that wasn't the only problem. I didn't want to look stupid or scared in front of my students. I didn't want to be halfway up that wall, immobilised by terror. One part of me said, 'I can do it because I'm not chicken'. The other said simply, 'If I do, I'll be sorry'.

Day Three of the Year Nine Outdoor Education Program. Abseiling. I stood on the oval and gazed up at the wall erected the day before. My Year Nine class were clustered eagerly around it, and I knew I would never be able to get to the top — ropes, harness, expert helpers notwithstanding.

'No, I'm not really scared you know. I suffer from vertigo.'

I rehearsed that line a few times in preparation for the inevitable invitation to climb the wall. Vertigo is very strange — the feeling slowly creeps through my body and grips me tightly. At the same time it is heady, as if the world is calling me to fall and fall and fall.

The students were nervous but they had a go — all of them. I stood on the ground, busily and obviously taking photographs.

'Come on Mr Mac, it's grouse.'
'That's okay, I'm taking photographs.'
'I'll hold the camera and you can have a go.'
'That's okay. I'm not really scared you know. I get vertigo.'

They were understanding. Sympathetic. Tolerant. They helped me, by not hassling me to go up the wall, but not hassling me when I didn't go up the wall and by accepting my inability as being another aspect of who I am.

3. Write the first version of your story in your *Mindworks Notebook*.

4. Work with a writing partner and revise your story.

5. Write the final version in the space provided.

6. After Douglas showed us his story we discussed a suitable title. Our suggestions included: Climbing the Wall, Scaling the Heights, The Wall of Fear, Barriers, The Wall, Another Brick in the Wall, Facing My Fear.

   Douglas decided on 'The Wall Of Fear' as the title which best captured the feeling he was writing about. Think of a title for your story and write it in the space provided.

Reflection

Telling stories about your own life is called 'personal narrative writing'. It has a recognisable pattern:

1 the scene is set;

2 the event is described;

3 the writer reflects on what happened.

Check Douglas' story to see if it fits this pattern.
Now check your own. Does *your* story follow this pattern?

FIVE STEPS TO WRITING A FIRST DRAFT

Date completed ....

Here are five steps which give you one way of writing a first draft. For this activity use the steps to write a biographical piece about an interesting event in your life.

In the future you can use the same steps for other writing tasks.

1 Work with a partner for this activity

Number five pages in your *Mindworks Notebook* from one (1) to five (5).

Step one, Page one
Finding a topic

Write a list of 5 events in your life that you'd be prepared to develop into a story to be shared with others. The events must be things that have happened to you or that you have observed.

For example, playing in a basketball grand final, breaking your leg, an accident, a concert or a fight.

Time allowed for this list is 2 minutes and 10 seconds.

Share your list with your partner. Decide which of these events you will write about today.

Step two, Page two
Collecting the information

Write the event you chose at the top of the page.

List (brainstorm) all your ideas and information about this event.

Time allowed for this brainstorm is 1 minute and 55 seconds. Work quickly.

Share your list with your partner.

Step three, Page three
Choosing a starting point

Write 5 possible beginning sentences for your story. These sentences are your reader's first contact with your story. They need to invite your reader to continue reading.

Time: 4 minutes and 6 seconds.

Share with your partner. Your partner is a sample reader. Ask which opening he or she found most inviting.

Step four, Page four
Making a start

Write your chosen sentence at the top of this page and continue writing the first paragraph.

Time: 5 minutes 44 seconds.

Read your paragraph to your partner.

Step five, Page five
Elaborating the story

Copy your opening paragraph on to this page.
Continue writing and finish the story.

Time: 12 minutes and 51 seconds.

2 Read the whole story to your partner and discuss what you both like about it and whether any changes would improve it.

3 Edit and proof read your story and then write it neatly in the space provided.

Reflection
How could you use this method in subjects other than English?

TRUE COLOURS

Date completed ....

Twelve Tinted Truths

- The human eye can distinguish two million colours; only 7 000 colours have names.
- Bright yellow or red increases pulse rate, blood pressure and respiration.
- We are attracted to food that is red, orange, peach, yellow, light and dark green, brown, tan and white.
- A red room will make you feel warm and a blue one will make you feel cool.
- Classrooms painted certain shades of yellow have been found to improve the work of school children. Other shades of yellow can induce nausea and are not used in the interior of aircraft.
- Our sense of time moves more slowly in a red room, faster in a green or blue room.
- Babies can distinguish colours when two or three months old.
- Up until the age of three most children prefer bright primary colours to pastel shades.
- Orange and yellow stimulate appetite.
- Most colour-blind people can see colour but confuse different hues, such as red and orange with yellow and green.
- More males than females are colour blind.

1. Choose colours to represent each of the following adjectives. Write or colour them in the space provided.

attractive
hardworking
joyful
athletic
ugly
angry
happy
forgetful
honest
lazy
anxious
graceful

depressed
hopeful
popular
fearful
generous
deceitful
critical
boring
loving
dreary
friendly
disruptive

2. Draw an outline * of yourself below and dress it in your true colours. Use ideas you have collected from doing the previous task to describe the 'real you'.

MY TRUE COLOURS

*A photograph may help you get an accurate outline.

Orange like the sun,
Warm and kind —
Violent and hot
When you look inside.
Pale green, so cool,
Calm and restrained.
Gentle and caring.
These colours are me, mate!

David

Opal mauve is a colour
That has meaning in my life,
The parts of me that can be
Deep down or on the surface,
My feelings towards other people,
Not of hatred,
But of love, happiness and life.

Electric blue shows a different life,
My moods, violence, unhappiness
And an uncaring side of me.

It shows a life so different
Some people don't even know it's me.
It can also show
the hatred I feel for someone.

They are completely different colours,
— reflecting my life well.

Melanie

3 Write a poem about yourself from your True Colours. Choose colours which show different sides of your personality. Shape your poem so that it fits in the palette below.

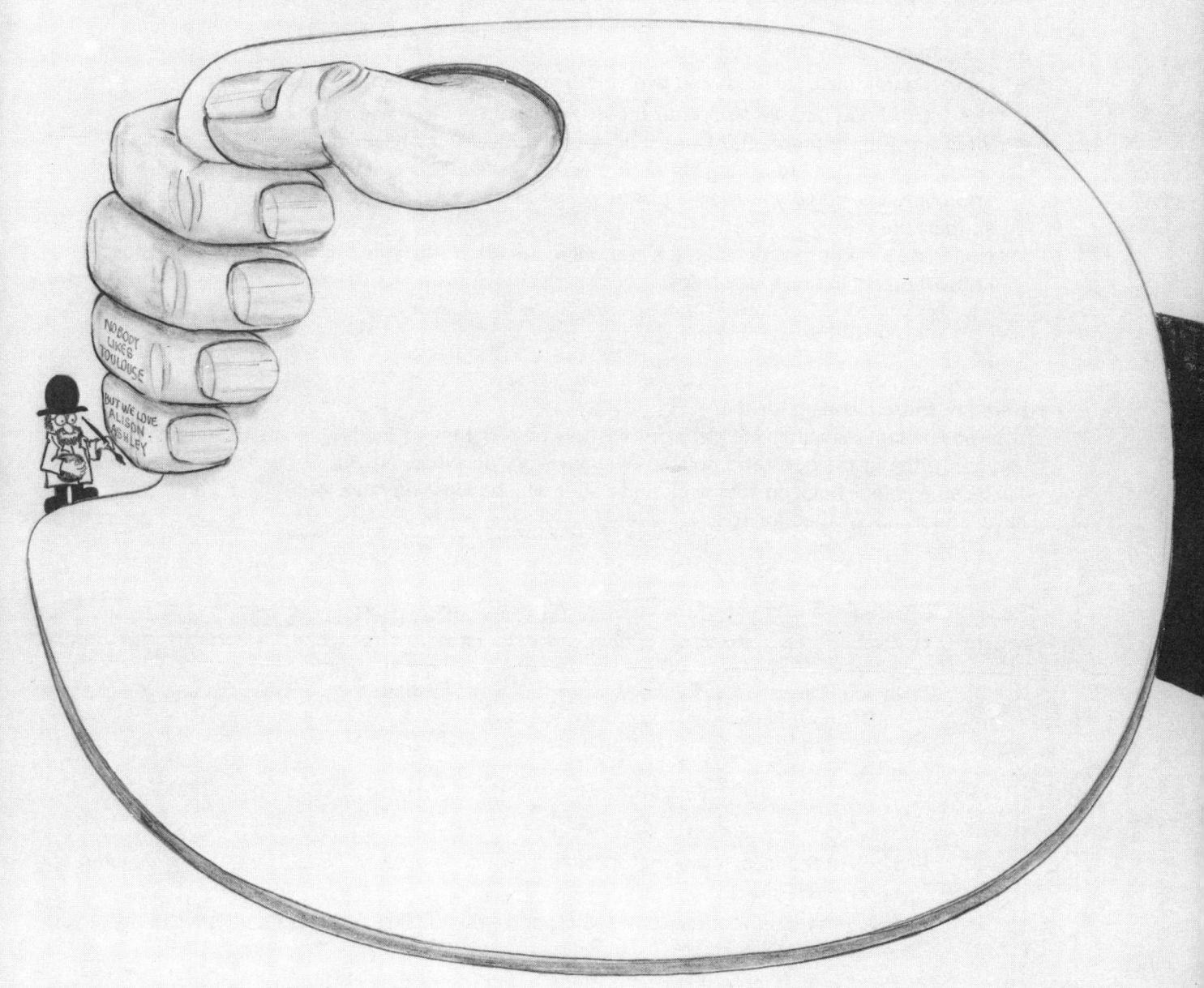

Something extra
Organise an out-of-uniform or rainbow day and come dressed in your favourite colours.

Reflection
Rate your work by colouring the eyes:
- blue for 'true blue' honesty;
- pink for 'white' lies;
- khaki for camouflaging your true colours.

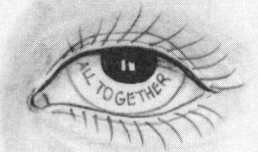

CREATING A MYSTERY

Date completed ....

By the time you reach this page you will have used several different approaches to writing, such as lists, maps, description, observation, fantasy, remembering and imagining.

You have also had experience at composing and presenting different kinds of writing such as poems, anecdotes, autobiography and fiction.

There are more to come but now is a good time to evaluate how you are growing as a writer, observer, thinker, editor and worker. Set aside some time to discuss your work with others, maybe in class, at home or elsewhere with people who are interested in you and in writing.

As a beginning follow these steps:
- Look though this book and read everything you have written in it so far.
- Use your *Mindworks Notebook* to record your answers to these questions.
What are your impressions? Does it all sound the same or have you written in a variety of styles? Is the book interesting? Is each piece complete and well presented? What improvements could you make? List as many as you can (ask other people to make suggestions).
Underline two improvements which you will focus when you write this next story. Write these improvements in the space below.

_____

_____

Here are more planning ideas
You may be familiar with these ideas or they may be new for you. In either case we suggest that you follow the instructions and notice how your story develops as you proceed. At the end you will be able to look back on your work and notice which ideas you have found useful and which have, so far, not worked for you.

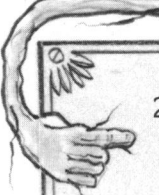

2. In your *Mindworks Notebook* write 15 leads * for this story. Choose the one you like best and write it below.

_____

_____

3. Look at the ideas in your story tree. In your *Mindworks Notebook*, write one paragraph about each idea.
4. Use the writing you have done so far and write the first complete draft of the story in your *Mindworks Notebook*.
5. Read your story to three other people and discuss it with them.
6. Write a second draft. **This time write each paragraph on a separate sheet of (scrap) paper.**

*A lead is often called an opening sentence. It is what *leads* the reader into your writing. Making yourself write 15 of these may not be easy but it is useful. It will get your brain working creatively and help you discover what you want to say and the best way to say it.

1 Develop the main ideas of your mystery story before you start writing. Complete each of the branches of the story tree by adding details.

What is the mystery (murder/treasure/ supernatural events/ disappearance of someone or something/other)?
Who is involved?
Where does it take place?
When does it happen (in the past, the present, the future or more than one)?
Why does it happen?
How is it solved?

As you think about the story, you may get ideas of other things to include. Use the extra foliage for these.

7 Shuffle the paragraphs around to find which is the most exciting and interesting way to arrange them. Paste them together in that order. Add new paragraphs where they are needed.
8 Proof read your story. Reading it aloud is best because you can then hear how well it flows. If it seems jerky or disconnected, rewrite the joining sentences to make it flow smoothly. Check that all spelling and punctuation are correct. Delete all unnecessary words. Be thorough in this task; it is a most important part of the writing process.
9 Rewrite the story on the following page with illustrations and colour. (Add another page if necessary.)

Something extra
Read your mysteries to each other in class and see if you can solve them before the story ends.

Reflection
Did your readers enjoy your mystery and how do you know? _____
_____

THE OTHER SIDE

Date completed ....

Have you heard the saying, 'There's more than one side to every coin'? Look at some coins and think about what this adage might mean.

WHAT'S AN ADAGE??

THIS DICTIONARY'S DEFINITION IS — 'AN OLD SAYING: A PROVERB.'

Danger

Beautiful things are dangerous,
The red, raging fire —
    the crackling flame,
The wild plunging horse —
    with flowing mane,
The swift, silent tiger —
    stalker in grass,
An Antarctic landscape —
    a frozen mountain pass,
The sharp, shining knife —
    cold gleaming blade,
And the sleek, spotted leopard —
    in sun-dappled shade.

Ugly things are dangerous,
The guileful crocodile —
    with big toothy grin,
The sleek, swift shark —
    eater of limbs.
The bristling wild boar —
    wily and old,
The swift-striking cobra —
    hooded and cold.
The lumbering rhinoceros —
    tank-like and horned,
And the small black spider —
    with red stripe adorned.

Melanie

Scary Things

Loud things are scary,
Like a scream of fear.
The shattering of glass,
Sharp and clear.
A clash of thunder,
On a cold winter's night.
The howling of a dog,
In the shimmering
    moonlight.

Quiet things are scary,
On a dark tranquil night,
The whistling of the
    wind,
The shivers, the fright.
The pavement is bare,
Faint footsteps behind.
The deadly silence,
Fearful thoughts in my
    mind.

Tracey

Moving Things

Moving things are beautiful;
The thundering charge of the
    buffalo,
A leaping, flickering fire — alight,
The crash and spray of a waterfall,
A draught-horse in harness so
    bright.

Still things are beautiful;
Dawn's soft mist adorning the hills,
Cold, bright comet in the starry
    deep,
Weathered sphinx resting ancient in
    the sand,
My baby sister asleep.

James

1. Complete each sentence in the pairs below with one of the adjectives from the list provided. **Use the same adjective for both sentences in each pair**. You will need to be able to explain your choice. Discussing it as you work will help you do this. How many adjectives can you use?

    Example: *Beautiful things are **necessary**.*
    *Ugly things are **necessary**.*

---

dangerous, beautiful, exciting, scary, inviting, challenging, loving, ugly, dynamic, harmful, useful, necessary, peaceful, threatening, marvellous

---

Beautiful things are _____   Loud things are _____

Ugly things are _____   Quiet things are _____

Cruel things are _____   Large things are _____

Kind things are _____   Small things are _____

New things are _____   Funny things are _____

Old things are _____   Sad things are _____

Swift things are _____   Easy things are _____

Slow things are _____   Difficult things are _____

---

2. Choose one of these pairs and work them into a poem which explains your idea. The poem will have two stanzas, each one giving examples of different things which share the one quality, such as *loudness*. The total poem will show how both loud and quiet things can be, for example, *exciting*.

3. Draft your poem in your *Mindworks Notebook*. An extra challenge is to write a poem for more than one of the ideas. This will give you a number to choose from before you decide which poem to include in this book.

4. Rehearse your poem privately and read it to the whole class before you copy it in here.
    If you get any feedback from your audience, or have further ideas yourself, make alterations to the poem and then write it in the space provided.

Something extra
Find the poem by Elizabeth Coatsworth called 'Swift Things Are Beautiful' which is the model for this activity.

Reflection
Are there more than two sides to every coin?

A DIFFERENT POINT OF VIEW

Date completed ....

When a photographer takes a photograph, an early step is to choose the point from which to view the subject.

Writers need to do this too.

For this activity the subject of the story is *you*: how you behave, what you are like, your positive and negative qualities.

The challenge is to see yourself from the point of view of one of your possessions.

1. List five possessions which 'see' a lot of you.

   _____
   _____
   _____
   _____
   _____

2. In your *Mindworks Notebook* write a brief paragraph about yourself from the point of view of **each** of these possessions.

3. Choose the paragraph or viewpoint you like best, or would feel happiest about recording in this book. Still in your *Mindworks Notebook*, rewrite it as the beginning of a description of the person who is you and **continue writing for 20 minutes**.

4. Re-read what you have written. Make any necessary changes or additions. Check that you consistently refer to yourself from your possession's point of view.

5. Write it in the space provided and illustrate it with pictures or photographs of you and/or the possession.

6. Give it a title.

Reflection
From this point of view, what kind of person are you?

Dear...

Date completed ....

Letters tell stories and stories can be told in the form of letters. Have you read any letters which tell stories of the past and of events in peoples' lives? One well-known Australian example is the 'Jerilderie Letter' from Ned Kelly. Can you think of any others?

The challenge for you now is to tell a story without giving any information except what is contained in the letters which two people send to each other.

This means your readers will need to 'fill in the gaps' between what is said in the letters and what has happened in the lives of the two characters. This is called 'reading between the lines'. Your task is to give your readers clues.

You will need portraits of two interesting people (not known to you). To find these, search through newspapers or magazines for pictures of the two characters who will write letters to each other in your story.

Choose pictures which will fit into the spaces provided.

PASTE PHOTO OF CHARACTER ONE HERE

NAME

PASTE PHOTO OF CHARACTER TWO HERE

NAME

1. In your *Mindworks Notebook* write a short biography for each character.

   Include the following information: name; age; date of birth; education; strengths; weaknesses; country of origin; country of residence; details of their family members, likes, dislikes, three important events in their lives; ambitions, occupation (if they have one); and any other details which occur to you.

2. From these biographies fill in the forms for both characters.

3. Decide the relationship between your two characters and which one of them will write first.

CHARACTER ONE

NAME: _____ AGE: _____

DATE OF BIRTH: _____ GENDER: _____

COUNTRY OF ORIGIN: _____ COUNTRY OF RESIDENCE: _____

DISTINGUISHING FEATURES: _____

OCCUPATION: _____

AMBITION: _____

FAVOURITE PASTIME: _____

CHARACTER TWO

NAME: _____ AGE: _____

DATE OF BIRTH: _____ GENDER: _____

COUNTRY OF ORIGIN: _____ COUNTRY OF RESIDENCE: _____

DISTINGUISHING FEATURES: _____

OCCUPATION: _____

AMBITION: _____

FAVOURITE PASTIME: _____

4 In your *Mindworks Notebook* draft six letters. Each letter is to be written from one character to the other, they may not necessarily write the same number of letters and they may not always reply.

   The letters may span weeks, months or years.

5 Copy these letters on to the kind of note paper that the writer could have used. Use different handwriting for each character.

   Staple the letters together in chronological order. Ask three people to read them and give you some feedback.

   Reader's names

6 Make any changes you think will improve the story and then attach the letters to this page.

Something extra
Have a class performance or make a tape recording with the letters being read in different voices to suit the characters.
or
Make a class display of your letters.

Reflection
What problems did you encounter doing this and how did you solve them?

_____

_____

_____

A BEAUTIFUL PLACE

Date completed ....

My Paradise

*A place of stunning beauty
A hill of fading light
A lyrebird displays his feathers
Another calls 'I might'.
The horizon lined with possums
Brilliant plants below
Tree ferns swaying softly
Rocking to and fro.
All around a peaceful breeze
Blows with gentle care
A wombat lumbers slowly
And looks up to sniff the air.
The tree-creepers sing cheekily
As they take small bites
Of moss and of lichen
And tiny gum-tree mites.
The creatures of the night appear
To feed beneath the stars
This marvellous place
This wondrous land
Is my paradise.*

Kate

Your memory contains the record of the sights and sounds of hundreds of different places. Open your *Mindworks Notebook* at an empty page and do the following:

1. Sit quietly and let the pictures of these places float through your mind. Search for the *most beautiful* one among these pictures.
2. Focus on this place — recall the colours, the sounds and the sights and re-create the feelings which it awakens in you.
3. On the page in front of you write down the things you see, hear and feel as they surface in your memory.
4. Write about this place beginning 'I wish I was there now'.
5. In the bubble on the opposite page describe this beautiful place.

Reflection

Who would you like to take with you when you next visit this place?

_____

_____

53

THE PERFECT GIFT

Date completed ....

1. On the opposite page you will see a box which contains the perfect gift for you. At the moment it is very plain.

   The kind of present in this box is not something you can buy. Nor can anyone give it to you.

   It is not something you can pick up and hold, but you can carry it around with you.

   It is something you can lose and find again and again.

   It is extremely valuable and no amount of money will buy it.

   It is a wonderful 'quality' or 'attribute' that you can make a part of yourself.

   It is something only you can give yourself.

2. Choose which of these qualities you will give yourself and put them in the box.

patience	intelligence
curiosity	creativity
confidence	application
perceptiveness	trustworthiness
intuition	fairness
wisdom	honesty
generosity	happiness
playfulness	sense of humour
tolerance	compassion
kindness	acceptance
bravery	reflectiveness
integrity	openmindedness

3. Using paper, pencils, stickers, glitter, ribbons and anything else you can think of, wrap this box beautifully so that the present is hidden. Attach a gift tag with your name on it.

4. The perfect gift for me is _____

5. Five ways this gift will change my life are:

   I will _____
   I will _____
   I will _____
   I will _____
   I will _____

6. I chose this gift today because _____

7. Four things I can do to develop this quality in myself are:

   I will _____
   I will _____
   I will _____
   I will _____

8. Ask a friend to suggest two more.

   I will _____
   I will _____

9   Read the following words aloud.
    *No one will ever give me this gift all wrapped up in a box.
    I have it now and can use it always.*

Something extra
The perfect gift for everyone in your class could be to stand in a circle and say these words ten times in unison.

Reflection
What is the best present you've ever given someone?

MINDWORKS CERTIFICATE

This is to certify that

_____

has completed _____/25 activities in this book

and has earned the following award:

Colour in this seal according to the award you think you deserve.

Check with your teacher and others if you would like a second or third opinion.

BLUE = your best work throughout the book.
RED = mostly your best work throughout the book.
GREEN = some of your best work throughout the book.

Dear Student,

We hope that you have enjoyed working in **Mindworks**. Take some time now to read through your book and identify the five exercises of which you are most proud. How will you identify them? With your special symbol drawn in your favourite colour.

These are our symbols:

We suggest you put this completed book away in a safe place for reading when you are older.

With best wishes for a lifetime of learning,

Rob, Sally, Douglas and Peta.